The Library Association

GW00630682

GUIDELINES FOR LIBRARY SERVICES TO PEOPLE WHO ARE HOUSEBOUND

Prepared by the
Domiciliary Services Subject Group
of the Library Association Medical, Health and
Welfare Libraries Group

and the
London Housebound Services Group
of the Association of London Chief Librarians

027.6
LIT

LIBRARY ASSOCIATION PUBLISHING
LONDON

© The Library Association 1991

Published by
Library Association Publishing Ltd
7 Ridgmount Street
London WC1E 7AE

First published 1991

British Library Cataloguing in Publication Data

Guidelines for library services to people who are housebound.
I. MHWLG Domiciliary Services Subject Group
II. Association of Chief Librarians. London
Housebound Services Group
027.6

ISBN 1-85604-029-1

Typeset in 10/12pt Palacio by Library Association Publishing Ltd
Printed and made in Great Britain by Amber (Printwork) Ltd,
Harpenden, Herts.

CONTENTS

page

Introduction   5

Summary of the Guidelines, including main
  recommendations   7

1   Criteria for eligibility to receive a housebound
    library service   13
2   Meeting the needs of key target groups   16
3   The funding and organization of the service   20
4   Staffing   27
5   Training   35
6   Assessment of users' needs   40
7   The visit   42
8   Services to residential homes, sheltered
    accommodation and day centres   44
9   Stock   51
10   Reading aids and tape services   57
11   Liaison with agencies   61
12   Promotion and publicity   65
13   Transport   70
14   Health and safety   74
15   Accommodation and equipment   77

Appendix 1   Membership of the working party   79

References   80

Sources of information and further reading   82

INTRODUCTION

A well-organized and effective housebound library service can make a major contribution to the quality of life for people unable to use library service points because of disability, illness, frailty, mental health problems, or their responsibilities in caring for others.

Library services are attempting to meet the challenge arising from the demographic changes within the population, which will result in a dramatic increase in the number of people living beyond 85 years. Although this is coupled with the fact that the overall number of elderly people within the population will begin to fall by the year 2000, there will be an increase in the oldest group, which experiences greater problems with mobility. The number of ethnic minority elders will also grow substantially. In London, for which figures are readily available, it will increase from 42,000 to 110,000 by the end of the century.

The development and promotion of community care policies by health care and social service providers will also bring about an increase in the number of people with disabilities living in their own homes with day care or domiciliary support. An important aspect of recent legislation, such as the Disabled Persons (Services, Consultation and Representation) Act 1986, and the National Health Service and Community Care Act 1990, arising from the Griffiths Report, is the emphasis given to the requirement to respond to leisure and social needs in individual assessment. Thus, many library services have attempted to introduce or expand their services to people with disabilities in the community, although even in similar authorities, provision is uneven. Additionally, the Green Paper 'Financing our public library service', elements of which were incorporated into the Local Government and Housing Act 1989, indicated a need for recognized standards of service in certain areas of library provision.

Existing documents which aim to give helpful information about housebound library services have been produced by the Library Association,[1] IFLA[2] and LAMSAC,[3] but they have either been found to lack sufficient useful detail, or are very specialized. This lack of suitable published advice for librarians wishing to introduce, or develop, services, led to the establishment, in September 1987, of a joint working party of the Domiciliary Services Subject Group (a sub-group of the LA Medical, Health and Welfare Libraries Group) and the London Housebound Services Group (an advisory subject group to the Association of London Chief Librarians).

The working party members were drawn from the two groups cooperating in the project, and involved librarians from London boroughs and shire counties, with experience of both staff-based and volunteer delivery services. Throughout the formulation of the document, other views have been sought and incorporated. The 15 sections were made available, in draft form, to specialist librarians, Chief Librarians and interested organizations and individuals, for consultation and comment. The final document was submitted to the Library and Information Services Committee of the Library Association for its approval and adopted by Library Association Council.

A fundamental concern of the Guidelines, emphasized by the order of the sections, has been to focus first on the user and then to progress to more technical points. For the purposes of this document, the term 'housebound' has been adopted throughout, because it is the generally accepted term for the services and user group described here. However, the document argues for provision of services which is wider than the term suggests. Also, the term 'staff' refers to paid and unpaid personnel.

Throughout the document, we have preferred to present ideas about serving people from ethnic minority groups in each section, rather than in one separate section, which we feel may marginalize their interests. At present, most housebound library services are making a minimal impact on these members of the community and we wish to encourage librarians to address their full range of needs.

Different options in organizing services are recognized, and the advantages or disadvantages are outlined where appropriate to reflect differing situations, structures and resources.

The aim of these Guidelines is to promote the effective use of resources, in order to achieve the best possible service to individuals within existing financial constraints, and to enable the housebound library user the same access to library services as those who use conventional service points. The final document represents a consensus of information and good practice.

The purpose of these ideas is that local authorities can use them to improve and develop services. How they are implemented will vary from authority to authority, and therefore it is at a local level that we expect valid performance measurements to be devised and applied.

SUMMARY OF THE GUIDELINES,
including main recommendations

Criteria for eligibility to receive a housebound library service
- The service should be made available to a wide variety of people who experience significant difficulty in using a library service point. Guidance is given on those sections of the community which will particularly need this form of support (1.1–1.4).

- The service must be flexible enough to provide for both temporary and permanent needs, and to recognize that each individual's situation will vary. Criteria for eligibility therefore provide a general basis for assessment of each individual application for service, but should be interpreted sensitively (1.5).

Meeting the needs of key target groups
- There should be a written general policy statement of aims and objectives for the service which describes long-term and current priorities and identifies key target groups, for each of which there should also be more detailed written service aims and objectives. These policies should be monitored by regular review of targets by senior managers in consultation with service delivery staff (2.1).

- Librarians must build up detailed information on demographic changes and issues of service policy and provision which will affect the demand for the housebound library service (2.2).

- The service should ensure that resources are reaching key target groups effectively, and that individual needs are being fully met, based on continuous feedback from users (2.3).

- The housebound library service must cooperate closely with other community and specialist library sections in the authority, with formal structures established where necessary to achieve this (2.4; 3.3).

The funding and organization of the service
- In setting up a new service, or reorganizing an existing one, careful

thought must be given to all aspects of funding need, including those elements of the service, notably transport, materials and equipment, which may be especially costly to provide (3.1).

- It is essential that the authority appoint a specialist coordinator to have authority-wide responsibility for the service, and that this person report to an authority-wide post to ensure that the service's needs are represented at policy-making level (3.2).

- Centralized and decentralized systems of housebound library service each offer both advantages and disadvantages, which are described. Whichever system, or variant of it, is adopted by an authority, its advantages need to be fully exploited in the organizational and management structures established (3.4).

- The location of the housebound library service should be considered carefully to ensure that its work can be carried out effectively (3.5).

Staffing

- Staffing provision should start from the premise that users of housebound library services require access to trained staff in the same way that general library users do, and this should not be denied to them simply because this level of service might be difficult or expensive to provide (4 – Introduction).

- The functions of the coordinator include a wide range of essential tasks and these are laid out (4.1).

- Depending on the local structure of services and authority policy, staffing options will include the use of specialist librarians and non-professional staff working only in the housebound library service, community library staff, volunteers, or a combination of all or some of these. Issues arising from these options are discussed (4.2).

- It must be recognized that a heavy dependence on volunteers will almost certainly produce limitations in the type of service provided, but, where they are used, they may have a valuable role, provided that they are working within a clearly defined framework and that arrangements are made for library staff to select, train and manage them (4.2.4).

- Because of the demands of the job, one person should not make more than 15–20 individual visits per day, nor make visits for more than four days in any week (4.4).

- Staffing levels should be calculated by using a formula which analyses the time spent in preparation, visiting, travelling, follow-up work and other base work. Guidance is given, where appropriate, on working out likely times for these duties and on applying the formula (4.5 – 4.6).

Training

- Formal and informal training, on an ongoing basis, is essential for all housebound library service staff, covering knowledge of systems, stock, client groups and agency roles, and communication and technical skills (5.1). Professional staff will need additional skills (5.2).

- Regular, structured training should be provided for all volunteers, covering all areas of their responsibility at an appropriate level, as outlined in the schedule (5.3).

Assessment of users' needs

- All applicants for the service should be visited by a professional librarian who will explain the service to them, decide whether they are entitled to it, according to agreed criteria, and assess their library needs (6.1.1 – 6.1.3). They should receive further professional visits at least twice a year to discuss the service they receive and to see if their needs have changed (6.2.1).

- A user profile should be drawn up for each person served, containing key information about stock and information needs, and personal and access details (6.1.4).

The visit

- The minimum frequency for visits should be at least every four weeks and these should be at a regular time on each occasion (7.1.1 – 7.1.3). There should be flexibility to provide for temporary needs and to make additional one-off visits (7.1.4 – 7.1.5).

- The basic length of time spent with the user should be, on average, between 10 – 12 minutes, but there may be a number of reasons why additional time will need to be allocated (7.3).

Services to residential homes, sheltered accommodation and day centres

- A service to establishments should endeavour to match the range and quality of service which users would get if they were able to reach their local library, and to meet their special needs (8.1). This should include provision of a wide range of stock, equipment, information, book-related activities for users and non-specialist resources for the use of staff (8.5–8.6).

- A librarian should carry out an assessment of each establishment, drawing up a profile of users' needs and liaising closely thereafter with the staff (8.2).

- The success of the service depends on maintaining regular access by users to trained library staff (8.3).

- Deposit collections and/or mobile delivery of services may be appropriate and guidance is given on providing each form as effectively as possible (8.4.1–8.4.2), and on how these may operate in relation to different types of establishment (8.7).

- It may be appropriate to provide transport to take people to libraries but arrangements of this sort need to be carefully planned (8.4.3).

Stock
- It is important that housebound library service staff are involved in stock selection, either directly in a centralized service or in an advisory role in a decentralized system (9.2).

- Users must have access to the same range of materials as individuals using a community or mobile library, both in terms of their general and their specialist needs, and this range is described in detail (9.4).

- The two usual methods of selection for the user are pre-selection of all items at the base library or taking boxes of material from which the user selects. Each has points in its favour and these are discussed (9.5).

- Users should be provided with sufficient material to last between one visit and the next (9.6). Steps should be taken to avoid users being given the same material more than once (9.7).

Reading aids and tape services
- Librarians should have a working knowledge of reading aids and how and where they can be obtained. Users who require more than a basic aid should be referred to a professional agency for expert advice and assistance (10.1).

- The service should provide a wide range of commercial talking books, together with the loan of cassette players and assistance with choosing from the catalogues of national tape library services. Librarians should have good knowledge of local and national talking newspapers, tape libraries, sources of taped information and other tape services, and should refer users to these as appropriate (10.2).

Liaison with agencies
- Cooperation with other agencies, whether on an informal basis or as part of a defined partnership, is essential if the service is to achieve its aims and enhance its provision. Good liaison can be mutually beneficial and achieve a variety of purposes, which are listed, if extended to a wide range of local and national agencies (11.1 – 11.2).

- Where another agency is involved in the provision of the housebound library service, effective liaison should include the development of a clear policy framework and formal arrangements for recruitment and training, stock selection and monitoring (11.3.1).

- With other agencies, liaison should take place in the areas of publicity, referrals of users, training, joint planning, joint activities and advice on stock selection (11.3.2 – 11.3.10).

Promotion and publicity
- Promotion should be used to create a favourable environment for the service by developing and advertising an image which is positive, attractive to potential users and multi-ethnic. This will include use of a wide range of printed publicity material, and a full programme of displays, talks to users, attendance at events and other activities (12.1).

- Printed, taped and broadcast publicity must be effectively distributed, using other local organizations and media, produced to a high standard in terms of content, language, visual images and production, and made available in formats and community languages which will be accessible to existing and potential users of the service (12.2).

Transport
- Decisions about choice and use of vehicles are of great strategic importance for the service. A range of factors needs to be taken into

11

account when selecting and operating transport, including size, facilities, finishing, garaging, insurance and maintenance arrangements. It is preferable that drivers should be under the direct control of the library service (13.1–13.6).

Health and safety
- The nature of work in the housebound library service may make staff and volunteers more vulnerable to illness and/or injury than building-based staff, and they must be trained in specific as well as general health and safety practices, for example in lifting and carrying correctly, use of equipment and vehicles, issues of stress and personal security, first aid and accident and insurance procedures (14.1–14.9).

Accommodation and equipment
- Those involved in the provision of accommodation for staff, and in its management, should have a clear understanding of the purpose and function of the service, including its requirements in terms of site/location, space, storage facilities and equipment, which are summarized (15.1–15.2.4).

1
CRITERIA FOR ELIGIBILITY TO RECEIVE A HOUSEBOUND LIBRARY SERVICE

The criteria (1.1–1.4) should be read in conjunction with the notes on interpretation (1.5) which follow.

1.1 The housebound library service should be available to people of any age who experience significant difficulty, for example through disability, in using a library service point. This includes not only libraries but mobile stops and outreach collections supplied to residential homes, sheltered accommodation, day centres and community groups.

1.2 Difficulty in using a library collection may be of a permanent or a temporary nature. People with a short-term need for a housebound library service (for example, through illness or accident, or because of seasonal factors), should be eligible for consideration.

1.3 The difficulty may arise for one of several reasons. A person may be unable to:

1.3.1 leave the home or other place of residence

1.3.2 travel to the library or collection

1.3.3 gain easy access to the library or collection (for example, because the building has poor facilities for users with mobility problems)

1.3.4 carry materials to or from the library or collection.

1.4 The people most likely to experience some or all of these problems are:

1.4.1 those who are elderly and frail or infirm

1.4.2 those with physical disabilities

1.4.3 those with sensory disabilities, especially severe visual impairments

1.4.4 those with profound or severe learning difficulties, especially where these are associated with physical or sensory disabilities

1.4.5 those with certain mental health problems (for example, agoraphobia) which make it difficult for them to leave the home

1.4.6 those suffering from illness, or recuperating from injury or operation

1.4.7 those who are 'culturally' isolated in the home

1.4.8 those who may be prevented from using library facilities while caring for any of the above, or because of other regular caring responsibilities

1.4.9 young children in the care of any of the above.

1.5 *Notes on interpretation of the criteria*

1.5.1 Criteria of this type can only provide the basis on which to make an assessment of each individual application for service, which would be fully considered at an initial interview, and through later reassessments (see Section 6 Assessment of users' needs).

1.5.2 The criteria cannot be applied rigidly to all people in similar situations. For example, many people with profound learning difficulties may be able to use library collections, depending on local transport facilities or the availability of support from families, social workers and other carers. Similarly, the same degree of visual impairment may handicap one person much more than another.

1.5.3 The underlying principle behind offering the housebound library service to such a wide range of potential users is that they will therefore have the right to choose materials for themselves rather than rely on a friend or relative to select for them.

1.5.4 Where a person is expected to use an outreach collection, rather than be taken onto the housebound library service, it is essential that the range and size of that collection should reflect the needs of its users.

1.5.5 The provision of a housebound library service should not be seen as a permanent arrangement for every user. People who have limited social or life skills, or who lack confidence, may need this type of personalized service for a while, but may then feel able to visit libraries for themselves. Many people who have been in institutions (for example, for people with learning difficulties, or mental health problems) may benefit from a housebound library service when they first begin living in the community, but only as a bridge by which they can be encouraged to make fuller use of the community's facilities, including library collections. Black people and those from other ethnic minorities, who frequently experience racial harassment, may be unable to leave the home easily or safely. Every possible support should be given to them, including the provision of the housebound library service where this is appropriate.

1.5.6 Overall improvements to library buildings (for example, access and design for people with disabilities) will also influence the extent to which some people will continue to need a housebound library service.

1.5.7 Librarians who effectively publicize a housebound library service to as wide a range of potential users as is envisaged in these criteria may well find that they are faced with more demand than they can easily meet. It may then well be necessary to consider prioritizing some people over others in the same category, or in different categories. To this extent also, written criteria are only a tool to establish an overall policy and consistent approach: only a personal interview can be sensitive enough to weigh one user's needs against another's, where the question of prioritization arises.

2
MEETING THE NEEDS OF KEY TARGET GROUPS

Introduction
This section deals with some general principles of service development to the key target groups of the housebound library service. These are groups which should receive particular attention if the criteria for eligibility to receive a housebound library service (Section 1) are interpreted as intended.

The groups are:

- elderly people who are frail or infirm
- those with physical or sensory impairments
- people with learning difficulties
- people with mental health problems
- carers.

Within each of these groups, the particular needs of black people and other ethnic minority communities should receive close attention.

A number of the general sections of this document deal with particular aspects of service provision as they directly affect users, particularly those within the key target groups. These sections (numbers 5–12 especially) contain a range of practical ideas, but we have not provided detailed guidance on service to each key target group. The reading list includes specialist library literature and other sources of information on work with these groups.

2.1 *Aims and objectives*

2.1.1 There should be a general policy statement of aims and objectives for the housebound library service which describes long-term and current priorities and identifies key target groups. It should reflect the overall policy of the library authority.

2.1.2 There should also be more detailed aims and objectives for services to each of these groups, highlighting within them the needs of people from ethnic minority communities and other minorities such as older or disabled gay men and lesbians.

2.1.3 These should be either:

- the authority's existing general Equal Opportunity Policy statement, if applicable, suitably developed to refer in more detail to the work of the housebound library service

or

- a policy specifically developed with children's and branch/community sections as relevant, for service to these target groups on an authority-wide basis.

2.1.4 These policies should be in written form and be regularly revised. Arrangements should be made for the monitoring of aims and objectives by regular review of targets by senior managers, in consultation with staff providing day-to-day services to housebound clients.

2.2 *Identifying current needs*

2.2.1 The most accurate picture possible should be built up of the numbers of people in each target group, and of changing demographic patterns. Housebound services librarians should be familiar with statistics such as those contained in Disabled Persons Registers maintained by Social Services Departments, and with other data, for example from local surveys.

2.2.2 Librarians should also be fully aware of Government and local authority policies as they affect provision for key target groups in their area, for example the impact of community care initiatives.

2.2.3 Close liaison with local agencies and organizations is essential in order to develop a full picture of the numbers and needs of key target groups. In the case of services to people with learning difficulties, for example, librarians should have contact with any strategic mental handicap planning groups for the authority, authority-wide support teams such as speech therapists, local Mencap societies and adult day centres, residential projects and educational and recreational groups such as Gateway clubs. See Section 11 Liaison with agencies, for further guidance.

2.2.4 Where there is limited information available about the numbers and needs of key target groups, contacts must be made with local organizations which have direct knowledge of clients. Leaders of churches and other places of worship, for instance, are an essential point of contact with ethnic minority elders who may need a housebound library service.

2.3 *Targeting resources*

2.3.1 The housebound library service should be continuously under review to monitor its impact on key target groups. The people being served at any time should be compared to the broader profile of the community. Where it is clear that certain groups are not being reached effectively, measures should be taken to increase the service's impact and additional publicity, stock and other resources made available to do this, or priorities reviewed.

2.3.2 The effectiveness of the service in meeting each individual's needs, based on requirements listed in the user profile (see Section 6 Assessment of users' needs), should also be monitored regularly. Additional resources such as stock or community information should be provided to meet special needs arising from disability or other factors.

2.3.3 Users should be encouraged to put forward their views about the service they receive and decisions about service development should be informed by these comments. Staff must be able to work with a great variety of people, both one-to-one and in organizations. They will increasingly come into contact with users who, for example, have profound learning difficulties or are experiencing mental health problems in old age. A high priority should therefore be given to equipping staff with the interpersonal and bibliographic skills necessary to provide an effective and non-patronizing service to all users. Training resources should be targeted accordingly (see Section 5 Training).

2.4 *Cooperation with other library sections*

The housebound library service should:

2.4.1 not operate in isolation from other library sections. There should be close cooperation, formalized through regular meetings, to provide a wide range of services to key target groups;

2.4.2 link with community libraries to arrange introductory library visits for members of these groups where this is appropriate. This could include visits for people with learning difficulties to give them opportunities to join, choose items and meet staff, and for people with mental health problems, recently discharged into the community, to help them to gain confidence in using local services and facilities;

2.4.3 work with community libraries to develop clubs and other library-based activities for isolated elderly people;

2.4.4 encourage people from key target groups and those who work with, or care for, them, to publicize their needs through the library service. Community libraries should cooperate to arrange displays and exhibitions, for example of work by individual housebound artists or photographs of, and information about, a day centre's activities.

3
THE FUNDING AND ORGANIZATION OF THE SERVICE

Introduction

As the introduction to these Guidelines underlines, housebound library services make a vital contribution to the lives of their users, which can be developed further still if given the necessary support. Despite this, the service may often be given a low priority, especially in the allocation of resources, and is therefore unable to do its work effectively.

To fulfil its role, it needs a place in the organizational structure of the whole library service which will ensure that it develops to its full potential, in close relationship with community and specialist services, as an equal partner in a fully integrated service. It also needs an adequate, separately identified budget, to provide the necessary resources.

Housebound library service staff have a specialist knowledge, especially regarding their users, which contributes to the pool of skills which go to make up an effective library service.

3.1 *Funding of the service*

3.1.1 A library service to housebound members of the community has the following major funding needs – staffing, stock, transport, accommodation, furniture and fittings, equipment, publicity and administration. In setting up a new service, or reorganizing an existing one, careful thought should be given to each of these areas. It is essential to balance the immediate needs with the likely longer-term needs of what will be a developing service.

3.1.2 Hidden costs, sometimes particular to operating a housebound library service, must be clearly identified so that the actual funding requirements of the service are accurately assessed and represented in the budget-making process.

3.1.3 Some elements of the service may be especially costly to provide, notably transport, materials and equipment.

- The library service to housebound users provides a wide range of materials, some of which, for example spoken word cassettes, highly illustrated non-fiction and specialist resources for reminiscence and group work, are usually expensive to purchase.

- The service may also provide users with items of equipment such as cassette players and bookrests, and these will require additional funding.

3.1.4 Extra funding to develop the service may be available from other sources within the general library service. It may, for example, be considered appropriate that the funding for some materials comes from other specialist budgets such as music, children's, local studies, reference or special services.

3.2 *Coordination of the service*

3.2.1 Focus for the housebound library service should be provided by the appointment of a coordinator who will have authority-wide responsibility and report to an authority-wide post (for example, head of lending services). In this way, the housebound library service's needs will be represented at policy-making level and the coordinator will be able to contribute at an appropriate point of the decision-making process regarding resource allocation and operational issues.

3.2.2 It is essential to have a specialist coordinator, in close contact with the delivery of the service, to ensure that all parts of the housebound library service are provided to the highest possible standards, and that these standards are consistent throughout the area served. The coordinator will be responsible for the monitoring and evaluation of the service to ensure that it continues to meet its objectives and the needs of the users. The coordinator also gives outside agencies a central point of contact within the authority.

This applies whether the service is organized on a centralized or a decentralized basis. However, it is also important in large, dispersed geographical areas, that users have local librarians with whom they can establish good contact.

3.2.3 The coordinator should be a professional librarian. His/her responsibilities may also include the coordination of general library services to elderly people and those with disabilities, or management of a section also serving hospitals and other establishments.

3.3 *Liaison with other specialist librarians/community library staff*

Because housebound library services should not operate in isolation from the rest of the library service, effective liaison, to exchange skills and information, is essential. This includes:

3.3.1 Liaison with other specialist librarians

- to improve housebound service staff's knowledge of other users and materials, for example, information about:

  - ethnic minority users, materials in community languages and multicultural stock
  - information about children and young people as readers, where they may be served by the housebound library service.
  - information about children's stock, including that which may also be appropriate to use with older adults, such as illustrated history books.

- to encourage specialist librarians to develop stock and information relevant to housebound people (for example, reference and local information on health topics of particular interest to elderly people and those with disabilities).

3.3.2 Liaison with community library staff

- to ensure that local knowledge of developments in the community, and referrals, are fed into a centralized service.

- to motivate community library staff to develop stock and information relevant to elderly people and those with disabilities.

3.4 *A centralized or decentralized system?*

It is not the purpose of these Guidelines to recommend one type of system rather than another. Many factors will influence the choice of system, including the size of the authority, the funding available, existing organizational models in the authority, and the level and scope of service to be achieved.

Possible models include:

- a fully centralized service, operated authority-wide from a single section

- a fully decentralized service, with all resources provided at local level but with overall coordination (as outlined in 3.2 above)

- a partially decentralized service, but with some centralized resources (for example, transport, stock) where economy or convenience dictate, and with overall coordination

Careful assessment of the advantages and disadvantages of each system is necessary. While local factors may influence the extent to which these advantages/disadvantages apply, some of the pros and cons of a centralized and a decentralized system would usually be:

3.4.1 A centralized service – advantages

- better overall coordination of policy, standards, systems, staffing, publicity

- allows pooling of scarce resources (for example, transport, equipment, garaging)

- concentrates expertise

- more likely to be seen as a service equivalent to other specialist sections because of concentration of resources to form an identifiable unit

- more effective representation of housebound users' needs because feedback and demands on the service are coordinated and can be translated into pressure for resources

- offers a convenient central referral point for the public and for agencies

- allows own stock to be built up over a period of time, improving staff's knowledge of materials and access to information resources on-site.

3.4.2 A centralized service – disadvantages

- may be insufficiently in touch with local needs

- if the service is based in a separate centre, of which it has sole use, the cost of running and maintaining the building will be higher than with shared accommodation

- longer distances to travel to users will result in higher costs for use of transport, and will also increase staff time used in journeys

- may produce over-reliance on own stock and lack of imaginative use of resources available elsewhere in the system.

3.4.3 A decentralized service – advantages

- involves a wider range of library staff and allows them to develop skills and interest in the service

- this experience feeds directly back to improve community library services to elderly people and those with disabilities since knowledge built up through the delivery of housebound library services (for example, special materials, awareness of mobility and access difficulties) can be applied to building-based and other community services

- improves take-up of the housebound library service since many housebound people have been library users and there will be continuity of service to them when they begin to require home visits. Potential users will have a direct line to local staff

- journey time to users will be shorter, and therefore savings will be made in staff time and other costs.

3.4.4 A decentralized service – disadvantages

- it may be more difficult to coordinate policy and maintain consistent standards across an authority where housebound library services are provided at local level

- it may prevent staff building up expertise in depth since work with housebound users may be a small part of their overall responsibilities

- the service may be seen to be dispersed and without focus unless the coordinator is able to develop a strong identity and clear referral systems

- it will be harder to identify the separate costs involved in providing the housebound library service

- where it is provided by community library staff as part of their regular duties, the needs of the housebound library service may be given a low priority.

3.4.5 However, while each type of system, or variation, will offer certain advantages, these need to be fully exploited in the organizational and management structures established so that any disadvantages are offset. For example, if it is decided that a decentralized service allows people to be served as part of their local community, through community libraries, effective specialist training and support must be provided for these staff to carry out their roles successfully.

3.4.6 Whichever system is adopted, it is essential that there is a communications structure which allows housebound library staff at all levels to feed in ideas, be involved in policy and stock selection decisions, and work within a clear management framework.

3.5 *The location of the housebound library service*

When establishing a new service, or reorganizing an existing one, the location of the section is one very important consideration. Clearly, if the service is fully decentralized, accommodation within community library or area facilities will have to be provided, taking account of the need for appropriate work space, storage areas and garaging for specialist stock, equipment and vehicles.

Where the service is centralized, however, managers would need to assess whether staff could work more effectively based in a large library or in a separate building or small library. Some of the pros and cons of being based in a large/central library include:

3.5.1 Advantages

- gives access to a wide range of general and specialist stock, and of reference and information materials from which to follow up enquiries from housebound users more quickly

- facilitates involvement in the wider and specialist structure of the library service by bringing housebound library staff closer to the overall operational centre

- improves access to other specialist librarians whose skills may readily be drawn on.

3.5.2 Disadvantages

- the housebound library service needs a clear and visible identity of its own and this may be submerged in a large, multi-function library

- housebound library staff need assured access to facilities and equipment (for example, bibliographies, microfiche readers) at all times and this may not always be available with shared resources

25

- housebound library staff may be drawn off to provide temporary staffing in other areas of the library unless a clear agreement is reached about their work priorities and responsibilities.

4

STAFFING

Introduction

Deciding how to staff a housebound library service is one of the most difficult and important of all those decisions which will have to be made, since it is on this that the rest of the service depends. The number of staff and the grades of staff depend on the type and quality of service being provided.

Issues covered in this section are:

- the role of the coordinator
- the advantages and disadvantages of using specialist professional staff, specialist non-professional staff, community library staff or volunteers
- the selection of visitors
- the level of staffing required.

The library and information needs of people who are chronically ill or who have disabilities are as wide as those of the general population. The difference between the two groups lies not in the needs but in the delivery of the service and the special formats required. The library user has access to trained staff on site. It would seem logical, therefore, since the library needs are no different, that users of housebound library services should not be denied this level of service simply because it might be difficult or expensive to provide.

4.1 *The role of the coordinator*

A professional coordinator is essential whether the service is centralized and run from one point to all delivery areas or whether it is operated in a decentralized form from a number of libraries. For the service to run efficiently and fulfil the needs of the readers there must be at least one professional librarian for whom it is of primary importance to develop, manage and promote the service.

The functions of the coordinator of any housebound library service should be:

4.1.1 to participate in the policy-making process

4.1.2 to ensure a regular and reliable service to users by making sure that the books and other materials, the visitors and the transport are available at the appropriate time

4.1.3 to ensure that the library needs of the users are assessed and re-assessed as required

4.1.4 to understand and to apply agreed criteria of eligibility in order to accept or decline applications for the service

4.1.5 to recruit the appropriate staff

4.1.6 to motivate and direct the staff

4.1.7 to support and counsel the staff

4.1.8 to ensure an adequate and continuing system of staff training in order to maintain and improve the quality of service provided

4.1.9 to ensure that appropriate and sufficient stock is available to meet the user's needs

4.1.10 to ensure the provision of bibliographical resources for booklists, spoken word cassette lists and other aids

4.1.11 to make available an information service to users by supplying leaflets and information, providing a referral service, and, perhaps, by initiating a newsletter

4.1.12 to promote and publicize the service.

4.2 *The staffing options*
The options are to appoint specialist librarians and specialist non-professional staff working only in the housebound library service, to use community library staff, or to use volunteers, or a combination of all or some of these. The course of action must depend on local factors. Relevant points to be considered are local resources for salaries, stock and transport, the geographical nature and extent of the region to be served and the attitude towards the use of volunteers generally, as well as their availability in a given area. The question of who should drive the vehicles must be addressed. There may be advantages in staff combining visiting and driving. The issues involved in having separate drivers are dealt with in Section 13.5.2 Transport.

4.2.1 Using specialist librarians

Librarians working in this way will have a full commitment to the service. They will have the chance to get to know the users and assess and meet their needs fully, to exploit the stock effectively and to develop the service as opportunities arise.

A professional service can be offered when visiting users, based on an in-depth knowledge of the stock immediately available and a broad knowledge of resources elsewhere in the library service. This should include community information. An awareness can also be developed of the role and resources of Social Services Departments and of other organizations working with elderly people and those with disabilities.

Reaching ethnic minority users needs particular attention. If, in a given authority, there is a substantial group of people using the same language or with the same cultural background, it might be considered necessary to appoint a librarian to work specifically with that group of people. In other authorities, where there are no staff appointed to work specifically with people from ethnic minorities, it is essential that staff in the housebound library service make contacts and develop stock knowledge which enable them to provide an effective service, and receive training to do this. In any type of authority it is the responsibility of every member of staff to develop an awareness of the needs of users from all cultural backgrounds.

4.2.2 Using trained non-professional staff as specialists

Staff need to be specially selected for the work, having shown an aptitude for the housebound library service. Well-trained non-professional staff can offer a good, regular and reliable service. They can utilize a growing knowledge of the users they serve and of the stock, even if they lack professional knowledge. With a librarian in post, complex enquiries can be dealt with competently and training to extend staff expertise can be continuous. Most staff will not be trained to a competent level in less than six months. It will be necessary to arrange for trained relief staff to cover for leave and sickness. Using community library staff occasionally can, in fact, be a useful means of promoting a more general awareness and understanding of the service.

4.2.3 Using library staff to run a decentralized service

One of the clearest advantages of operating a service from local libraries is that housebound users are seen as an integral part of the community.

Working in a service of this kind provides opportunities for community library staff to develop new skills and, if continuity of service is possible, to get to know local housebound users. A good decentralized housebound library service relies on there being someone on the staff who has been trained in this aspect of library work and also on an interest and commitment from senior staff.

A good service requires much more than just visiting the users with a selection of library materials. A lot of background work is necessary to enable staff to understand and satisfy users' expressed and, often, unstated needs. This involves a broad knowledge of library stock and resources and referral possibilities – something which it is not always possible to acquire in a decentralized service, where the work may be a very small part of a person's responsibilities.

4.2.4 The use of volunteers

A housebound library service run entirely by volunteers must be unacceptable to the library profession. Volunteers, however, may have a valuable role in service delivery provided that the library authority clearly defines the objectives, policies and organization of the service where volunteers are involved. Using volunteers is not an easy option and it may be difficult to recruit suitable people. If volunteers are to be used they must be carefully selected, trained, supported and supervised by a professional librarian. While volunteers may be able to give additional time to the visit, it is essential that they understand that their primary role is to provide a library service to the user.

It is very important that selection of volunteers is made by the librarian. Assumptions should not be made that a member of a particular organization can automatically become a library visitor. The line of responsibility must be clear so that when on library duties, problems, requests and information needs are reported to the librarian rather than to the volunteer organizer.

Problems which arise when utilizing voluntary helpers tend to be due to lack of supervision, proper training or monitoring. It is very important that users can depend upon the service to be regular, reliable and successful in supplying their library needs.

Finally, because of the nature of the role, it is very difficult for voluntary helpers to be aware of the vast range of stock and resources available. It has to be recognized that heavy dependence on volunteers will almost certainly produce limitations in the type of service provided.

A policy statement on the use of volunteers was produced by the Medical, Health and Welfare Libraries Group for the Library Association in 1987 and this should be referred to for more detail.[4]

4.3 *The selection of the visitor*

Whether they are paid staff or volunteers, the selection of the people who make visits should be done with great care. In any authority, efforts should be made to recruit from as wide a cross-section of the community as possible, including people from different cultural backgrounds, in order to reflect the needs of the community as a whole.

Points to be taken into account include that visitors should:

4.3.1 have the right sort of abilities and attitude for the job, which can be physically and emotionally demanding

4.3.2 have a good general interest in books and other library materials

4.3.3 be good at listening and communicating. Users often find it difficult to be articulate about their reading and/or listening needs and will also raise with the visitor many other needs

4.3.4 be able to work as part of the team and to communicate with others working in the service

4.3.5 show a commitment to the service. Training takes about six months for full-time staff if it is to cover the stock, the users and the basic referral requirements. Equally important, users of the service respond to continuity

4.3.6 be physically capable of doing the job.

4.4 *Demands of visiting*

4.4.1 Because of the physical and emotional demands of the job, we recommend that one person should not make more than 15 – 20 individual visits per day.

4.4.2 For the same reason, no person should be out visiting for more than four days per week at the maximum.

4.4.3 Two staff may be required to make some visits, either because of exceptionally heavy loads, a threat to personal safety, or driving and parking difficulties.

4.5 *Staffing levels*

Staffing levels must depend upon the number and distribution of people to be visited, the frequency and length of the visit, the level of service offered and the demands of the users.

31

The staff time required for serving housebound users can be divided into five parts:

- preparation for the visit
- the visit
- travelling time
- follow-up to visit
- other base work.

4.5.1 Preparation for the visit
This will include selection of items according to the user profile, including available reservations, and putting into bundles if pre-selection is in operation; selecting items and putting into containers according to genre if selection is made by the user during visit; loading onto the delivery vehicle.

4.5.2 The visit
Staffing levels will depend on the number of people to be visited, the frequency of the visit and the length of the visit. These are policy decisions which will affect the number of staff required. The previous recommendations that no staff member should visit more than 20 people a day, or go out on routes more than four days a week, will have a bearing on the calculations.

4.5.3 Travelling time
Travelling time between calls and the time required to get from base to the first call and back from the last, must be added to the visit time. This will vary very much according to the geographical spread of the calls and the type of area covered. An urban route with calls within a small geographical area will take less time than a spread-out rural route with the same number and length of calls. An inner city route, whilst geographically covering a small area, will have physical problems which will extend the travelling time, notably traffic and parking problems and reaching people living in high-rise flats.

4.5.4 Follow-up to visit
This will include discharge and shelving of items from the previous round; making amendments to user profiles; dealing with reservations and enquiries.

4.5.5 Other base work
Finally, add to this the time for stock selection, staff training, meetings, general authority commitments, annual leave and sickness. Time

should also be allowed here for informal discussion and support between staff.

4.6 *Formula for calculating staffing levels*

4.6.1 Once certain factors have been determined, a simple formula for calculating the number of staff required to serve any number of users can be used. The factors to be determined are:

- number of users to be visited
- frequency of visit
- average length of visit
- average travelling time between calls
- method of selection of material.

There are two parts to the formula. The first part gives a calculation for the actual time out en route (i.e. the visits), and the second part gives a calculation for the supporting base work.

4.6.2 Route times
Take as an example 20 users to be visited, where the frequency of visit is three-weekly, the average length of visit 10 minutes and the travelling time approximately 5 minutes between calls with 15 minutes to and from base.

The time taken to visit 20 users can be calculated by adding the visit time (10 minutes) to the travelling time between calls (5 minutes) plus the time taken to travel to and from base (30 minutes).

Calculation : $(20 \times 10) + (19 \times 5) + 30 = 325$ minutes
= 5 hours 25 minutes to visit 20 users

4.6.3 Supporting base work times
Calculations must be made for preparation of material, follow-up from the route and other base work to give the total staffing time required. Preparation and follow-up time can be calculated at an average of 14 minutes per user, where pre-selection operates.[5] If materials are not pre-selected, then time must be allowed en route for selection from the boxes of genre material to take in to the user – 5–7 minutes,[6] in addition to the time required for selection of material into boxes for loading at base. It should be noted that the average visit time may have to be extended where pre-selection does not operate, as some users may take longer than 10 minutes to make their selection.

4.6.4 If, then, preparation and follow-up time is calculated at 14 minutes, for 20 users 4 hours 40 minutes should be added to the 5 hours 25 minutes route time, giving a total time of 10 hours 5 minutes. A calculation for other base work previously mentioned would need to be added. This has not been calculated here as the time will vary according to individual authority arrangements.

4.6.5 Using this basic formula it is possible to determine, with adjustments for local circumstances, how many staff are required to serve a given number of users. In the example given above, it has been assumed that only one person goes out on the route, but in some situations it may be sensible for two staff to work together. Travelling time is saved, for example, where users are clustered at one location and two staff can make the necessary visits in half the time. Security and safety may be another reason for pairing staff.

5

TRAINING

Introduction

It is important to note that housebound library service staff and volunteers often work alone in the community and have no immediate access to facilities which other staff take for granted. They need a thorough grounding in the full range of library services and should be adequately prepared for work within the community, with a good knowledge of local networks. Staff need to understand the library authority's responsibilities to users and the role of other agencies, to be aware of the appropriate lines of referral and have the ability to exercise judgement in use of them. Senior staff should be able to give support to staff working with housebound users and provide opportunities for discussion of problems arising from the nature of the work.

It is essential that staff develop their knowledge of disability awareness and communication skills. Wherever possible, people with disabilities should be involved in any training programme in order to improve interaction with users and potential users.

Staff must be able to operate appropriate aids, equipment and vehicles, and must also be aware of safe working practices, especially in relation to lifting and carrying materials.

To make the contact with users effective and helpful, staff also need training in visiting skills and other interpersonal skills to promote positive attitudes, give confidence and reduce the possibility of over-involvement with a vulnerable clientele. This can prevent staff assuming inappropriate roles and help them to develop the ability to recognize situations in which they cannot help and to refer.

The attached training schedule should help develop the skills required in library staff working in housebound library services. Some topics can be dealt with in a formal way but many are only developed through practice or the guidance of experienced staff. Managers will need to assess the level of training on these topics which is appropriate for their staff, depending on their knowledge, experience and needs.

5.1 *Training needs for all housebound library service staff*

5.1.1 Sound knowledge of library systems and services available from the housebound library service.

5.1.2 Sound basic knowledge of stock and how it can be used.

5.1.3 Sound knowledge of library systems and services available from other service areas such as Reference, Local Studies, Music, Drama and Children's.

5.1.4 Sound knowledge of referral and request systems for materials and information.

5.1.5 Understanding of ageing and disability and their effects, especially in relation to the use of library materials.

5.1.6 Interpersonal skills including visiting skills, handling and storing confidential information and coping with occupational stress.

5.1.7 Lifting and carrying equipment and materials.

5.1.8 Knowledge of relevant local agencies, their areas of responsibility and lines of referral, for example:

- Social Services Department
- National Health Service
- voluntary organizations.

5.1.9 Knowledge of relevant national agencies and services which:

- provide complementary services such as Talking books, large print services, Talking newspapers

- provide a range of services of a general nature, and information, for example the Disabled Living Foundation or the Spastics Society.

5.1.10 Acquisition of basic skills in communication with people who are:

- deaf or otherwise hearing impaired
- visually impaired
- physically disabled

or who have:

- learning difficulties
- mental health problems.

5.1.11 Cross-cultural communication skills.

5.1.12 Use of equipment and reading aids.

5.1.13 Driving skills as required.

5.2 *Additional training needs for professional staff*

5.2.1 Information skills and knowledge of specialist materials, information sources and systems.

5.2.2 Assessment of users.

5.2.3 Recruitment, training and support of staff and, where appropriate, volunteers.

5.2.4 Training for trainers.

5.2.5 Management of stress/counselling skills.

5.3 *Training for volunteers working in the housebound library service*

5.3.1 As recognized elsewhere in the document, housebound library services using volunteers for deliveries will be more limited in scope than those using trained staff. Therefore training should be structured and relate directly to the tasks that volunteers are able to perform.

5.3.2 The training programme should be devised to provide initial, basic and continuous training in appropriate skills.

5.3.3 Volunteers must be selected by the appropriate librarian, with a view to aptitude and ability. A commitment to the training programme must be made by the volunteer at the initial interview.

5.3.4 Initial briefing
After acceptance new volunteers should have a briefing session which explains fully the tasks they will carry out within the service. At this stage, the training programme should be outlined.

5.3.5 Basic training
This should be carried out in a series of sessions, within a given period. Sessions should not be longer than three hours. This recognizes that there are often other demands on the volunteer's time, and the likely receptiveness of individuals who may not have previous experience of library work or service objectives. The topics covered should include the following, at an appropriate level:

- sound knowledge of relevant library systems and services available from the housebound library service, and of lines of referral
- awareness of stock and how it can be used
- knowledge of services available from other service areas such as Reference, Local Studies, Music, Drama and Children's
- understanding of referral and request systems for materials and information
- understanding of ageing and disability and their effects, especially in relation to the use of library materials
- interpersonal skills, including visiting skills, handling and storing confidential information and coping with occupational stress
- lifting and carrying equipment and materials
- knowledge of relevant local agencies, their areas of responsibility and lines of referral
- appropriate knowledge of relevant national agencies and services
- acquisition of basic skills in communication with people who are:
  - deaf or otherwise hearing impaired
  - visually impaired
  - physically disabled

  or who have:
  - learning difficulties
  - mental health problems
- cross-cultural communication skills
- use of relevant equipment and reading aids
- driving skills as required.

5.3.6 Trained library staff should accompany volunteers on their first visits, to give confidence and ensure that training to date has been effective.

5.3.7 Continuing training
This is important in order to respond to training needs highlighted while monitoring the work of volunteers. It should also be used to keep volunteers up to date with relevant library activities.

In some library authorities a newsletter for volunteers is produced, and this can be helpful in informal training.

Volunteers should attend formal training sessions at least twice a year after the basic training programme has been carried out.

6
ASSESSMENT OF USERS' NEEDS

6.1 *Initial assessment*

6.1.1 Applicants should be visited by a professional librarian who will explain the service to them, use the agreed criteria, based on a locally adopted policy, to decide whether they are entitled to it, and assess their library needs. An initial assessment is necessary, even when the reader has been referred by Social Services or hospital staff.

6.1.2 For people whose first language is not English, it is important that, where necessary, the assessment visit is made by someone with appropriate language skills. This would be a member of library staff with, if necessary, a worker from another agency. Additionally, where it is important to give confidence to an applicant that the assessment will take full account of their needs, a visit may be made by a member of library staff with a shared cultural background.

People with disabilities may require that an interpreter or advocate be present at the assessment interview.

6.1.3 Assessment should be by a personal visit and by appointment. Library staff should carry an identity card. The various types of materials that the library service has to offer should be described, and examples shown. Samples of stock, including large print, periodicals, records, music and spoken word cassettes and videos, should be taken to give the applicant an idea of the range of stock available. Community information should also be brought to the applicant's attention. Because of their isolation, housebound people may not be fully aware of the wide range of services available in the community to which the library service can refer them. This may apply especially to people from cultures where services of this type are rare.

6.1.4 A record of the user's needs is essential. A user profile should be drawn up at the time of the initial assessment. This will give the service a current and accurate picture of what the user wants, and continuity when the service is delivered by different members of staff. While each authority's approach will reflect local priorities, any profile must contain a number of essential elements. These include information about:

- stock and information needs, for example range of materials, special formats, language(s) required

- user's disability (if any), as it affects library needs and communication

- personal and access details, for example, user's name, address and telephone number, how to gain entry, day and time for visit.

User profiles contain sensitive personal information and must be kept secure to safeguard confidentiality. Services which are computerized are additionally subject to the requirements of the Data Protection Act 1984.

- Contacts: details of referring agency, if any, and contact persons in an emergency.

Examples of profiles in use can be found in *Library services to housebound people*[7] and *A future age.*[8]

6.1.5   The user should be told the date of the first visit, and given details of how to contact the librarian and the name of the person who will be delivering the materials. Phone contact between the user and a contact member of staff should be encouraged.

6.2 *Continuing assessment*

6.2.1   Users should receive a professional visit at least twice a year to discuss the service they receive and to see if their needs have changed.

6.2.2   If the user has become more mobile, s/he should be encouraged to return to use of a library service point. If using a community library for the first time, the housebound library staff should help by explaining library procedures in advance.

7
THE VISIT

7.1 *Frequency of visit*

7.1.1 A regular frequency for visits should be established to give continuity and efficiency in the service.

7.1.2 We recommend that the minimum frequency should be at least every four weeks, and users should be allowed sufficient material to last until the next visit.

7.1.3 A regular time should be established for visits to each user. Many housebound people live alone and are vulnerable. Regularity helps to give them confidence in the identity of the caller, to be prepared for the visit, and to plan appointments (for example, hospital visits).

7.1.4 The service should also have the flexibility to provide visits to people with a temporary need – seasonal factors (for example, people who need the service only in winter) or temporary illness or injury.

7.1.5 Some users will require more frequent visits. The service should be flexible enough to cope with changed user needs, by providing additional one-off visits, for example, where a person is going into hospital and needs a supply of reading material, or has urgent requests.

7.2 *Content of visit*

7.2.1 Delivery of library materials.

7.2.2 Help and advice to the user in making a selection from the range available (where a wider choice is offered).

7.2.3 Feedback from the user on the materials provided (where pre-selection operates).

7.2.4 Noting of requests for materials.

7.2.5 Dealing with requests for information.

7.2.6 Passing on to the user information about the range of library and other services available.

7.2.7 Issue and discharge of material (if applicable).

7.2.8 Notifying the user of the date of the next visit.

7.3 *Duration of visit*

7.3.1 We recommend that the basic length of time for a visit (i.e. time spent with the user) should be, on average, between 10 and 12 minutes.

7.3.2 However, the service should be flexible enough to provide more time for users who may require a longer visit, for example:

- where a person has reduced mobility

- where a user may take longer to choose materials (for example, where there are language differences or where a person takes longer to express his or her needs)

- where there is more than one user in a household

- where the visitor needs to provide help in unforeseen circumstances (for example, emergencies).

8

SERVICES TO RESIDENTIAL HOMES, SHELTERED ACCOMMODATION AND DAY CENTRES

Introduction

The library and information needs of many people who are elderly or physically disabled, or who have mental health problems, and who would qualify for a housebound library service, may be served through the establishment in which they live (residential accommodation), or which they regularly attend (day care).

Residential accommodation

There are many types of accommodation in which people live on a group basis, where varying degrees of care are offered according to residents' needs. They may be residential homes or hostels, nursing homes or sheltered housing units. Such establishments vary in size from a few, to several hundred, residents. A small private residential home may house fewer than 10 elderly infirm people, but a sheltered housing complex may house 50 or more people under one roof in self-contained flats with communal lounges, surrounded by bungalows housing many more. Establishments may be owned by private individuals or companies, by charitable or voluntary bodies, by local authorities, by the health service, and by housing associations.

Day care

Some people may only be able to continue to live in their homes with the support of community care, through attendance at day centres for those who are elderly or have disabilities, mental health problems or learning difficulties. A range of services and activities is offered, designed to meet the physical, social and, possibly, the educational needs of clients, whose attendance may be daily or several times a week. They may accommodate as few as ten people a day, or as many as 100 or more, with a weekly clientele in excess of 300–400.

There is a very wide diversity of types, and of sizes, of establishment, for a range of client groups. In any one centre there may be clients with a wide range of disabilities. The needs of clients will determine the range of library service offered, and the method of service delivery.

The library and information needs of those living in, or attending, establishments are as wide and diverse as those of the general population. There may be a greater need for, and greater use of, the library service as these groups tend to have more leisure time. For many, the ability to use books will be affected by their level of physical and mental ability and a comprehensive range of print substitutes and information about reading aids should be part of the standard service. They may also have library needs related to their disabilities or to activities carried out in the centre.

The service

8.1   A service to establishments should endeavour to match the range and quality of service which users would get if they were able to reach their local library, and to meet the special needs arising from their disability. The elements that need to be considered are:

- assessment visit
- staff
- stock and equipment
- range of services to be provided
- form of service delivery.

8.2   An assessment visit should be made to determine the needs of residents and the method of service delivery. This should be carried out by a librarian, who will discuss the proposed service with the officer-in-charge, and talk to individual residents about their reading and information needs.

8.2.1   It will be necessary to draw up a profile of the establishment, and its library users. It will contain such details as name of owner and manager of the building, number of residents or clients, type of establishment, vehicular access, activities that take place, reading and information needs of residents, and of staff. It should be regularly updated.

8.2.2   Once the service has started, regular meetings should be held with staff to discuss issues of mutual interest and to ensure that the library service continues to play a full part in the life of the organization.

8.2.3   When a number of establishments operated by the same organization are being served, for example a service to a number of residential homes for elderly people operated by a Social Services Department, it is advisable to have occasional meetings at senior

45

management level to discuss issues which arise.

8.3 *Access to staff*
Users require regular contact with trained library staff if their needs are to be adequately met. The librarian promotes and stimulates library use, and is able to interpret users' needs so that satisfactory materials can be provided. The librarian will have the skills required to assist with the selection of materials for the user, and to advise on the appropriate use of materials and aids for people with all types of disability.

A successful service depends on maintaining regular access by readers to trained library staff, although the frequency will vary according to the needs of users and method of delivery.

8.4 *Service delivery*
Service delivery falls broadly into two types, static and mobile. The size and type of establishment will usually determine the method of service and the specific needs of users may result in a combination of methods of service.

8.4.1 The static deposit collection with all or part of its contents exchanged at intervals cannot work effectively without the input of trained staff to exploit the collection, encourage its use, and to make sure it continues to reflect and extend the interests of its users. The content of the collection should be sufficiently varied in scope and size to cope with the requirements of users. There should be exchanges at sufficiently frequent intervals to ensure a regular turn-over of stock.

Some establishments will require more frequent exchanges than others. It may not be possible to meet the needs of all users, or readers with specialized interests, from a deposit collection, and it may be necessary to supplement the collection with the housebound library service for specific individuals.

When considering a deposit collection as a means of service delivery, attention should be given to the potential number of users and sufficient material should be included to ensure that all will have enough material of interest to last between one exchange and the next. This is the determining factor when calculating numbers of books and frequency of exchange. For this reason, recommendations on size of collection and frequency of exchange in relation to the size of establishment are not given here.

Deposit collections may not be the preferred method of service delivery in establishments where the number of users is fewer than 10. They can be used quite satisfactorily in establishments with large numbers of library users, as long as the collection is big enough, adequately housed, and has a high level of staff input.

8.4.2 The mobile delivery of services has many built-in advantages. There is always staff contact at the point of service, and vehicles generally hold larger and more varied stocks than deposit collections. Vehicles vary in size and type – purpose-built mobiles (bookbuses) with a shelf stock of 1,800 items, with wheelchair lift and trolley that can be taken into establishments; conventional mobiles, usually larger than the bookbus; small vehicles holding 300–400 items and intended to support deposit collections. An authority with a larger number of institutions to serve, with a wide variety of client groups, may use all these types of mobile delivery, plus deposit collections, used singly or in combination, to give adequate delivery of services.

The pattern of visiting must be regular and according to an agreed timetable. The frequency and length of visit will vary according to the needs of users, but should not be less than monthly. The visit should be of sufficient length to accommodate everyone who wishes to use the service. Some users will not be able to get onto the vehicle and will have to be served from a trolley wheeled into the building, or sought out individually with a selection of material. For more detailed discussion of vehicles see Section 13.

8.4.3 Some library authorities provide transport to 'bus in' users who are unable to get to a library by their own efforts. A vehicle may be purpose-built for passengers, with wheelchair access, or a multi-purpose vehicle, which can be adapted for the occasion. Some authorities have their own vehicles, others use suitable borrowed transport from Social Services Departments or other agencies. The main advantage of this approach is that users have equal access to the full range of library services, and can choose their own material. This service can only be used successfully by people who have sufficient mobility and energy to get round the library shelves largely unaided. Staff will be required to help people on and off the vehicle, and into the library, and to give assistance within the building if required. The staff time and effort involved in organizing this type of service should not be underestimated. Particular attention must be paid to the safety of users whilst in the care of library staff, and this will involve drawing up safety guidelines to be followed. A rigorous examination should be made of the library, inside and out, to ensure that access for people with disabilities is adequate.

8.5 *Stock and equipment*

In addition to a wide range of fiction and non-fiction material, some or all of the following will be required – large print, taped books, newspapers and magazines, picture books, local history books and photographs, music, slides, jigsaws, games, puzzles, quiz books and materials for special groups such as people with learning difficulties. Reading aids and equipment, such as bookrests and cassette players, may be provided.

8.6 *Range of services*

8.6.1 Request, reference and information services and community information should be provided. There should be provision for referral to other agencies, for example consumer advice and national services covering all types of disability.

8.6.2 Many people will be unable to benefit from using books themselves, but will enjoy and be stimulated by book-related activities, for example reminiscence, story and poetry readings. Other activities which support the work of the establishment may also be offered, for example slide shows and films, or the materials may be provided for the staff of the establishment who will carry out the activities. If the librarian is involved in organizing additional activities, such as reminiscence sessions, then extra time must be found.

8.6.3 A service should be provided to establishment staff for their professional needs, to supplement specialist information and training resources from the Health Authority or Social Services Department. These will be two fold. Firstly, for materials from general library stocks to improve skills in caring for elderly people and people with disabilities, and to update their professional knowledge. Requested material should be provided, together with booklists and displays on topics in their field of interest. It may also be possible in large establishments, or on mobile vehicles, to provide collections of appropriate material. Secondly, for materials in support of organized activities for clients – books on crafts, quiz books, song books, games, music, photographs, slides, films and play sets.

8.7 Establishments and service delivery – some guidelines and examples

8.7.1 Day centres

Day centres may vary in size from fewer than 25 to more than 100 clients per day. Attendance by each client may be daily, or on one or several days in the week. Visits by library staff should be several times a month, on different days, so that each client has contact with a librarian at least once a month. The length of visit should reflect the number of people requiring the service, and their situations. Many people will have to be sought out in craft rooms, and many will need assistance with the selection of materials. At least one hour should be allowed for 10 – 20 library users. In large establishments, with active users, two to three hours may be needed, with extra time allowed in establishments where users require a high degree of assistance.

The bookbus may be the best method of service delivery. After clients have made their selection from the bookbus shelves, the trolley can be taken round the establishment for those who are confined indoors to choose their books. It could be supplemented by a deposit collection if necessary.

It may be possible to service a day centre using a large deposit collection, with regular staff visits as noted above. The collection should be exchanged regularly, not less than quarterly, and supplemented by requested materials at each visit. Particular care will be needed to match the content of the collection to the needs of users.

8.7.2 Residential and nursing homes

These vary in size from 10 to 70 or more beds, and they differ considerably in the mental and physical abilities of residents. For example, a nursing home with highly dependent and confused residents is unlikely to have many readers compared with an establishment of the same size where the residents are mentally alert, and this needs to be taken into account when considering service delivery. Depending on user needs, a deposit collection will be adequate for one establishment, but a bookbus service will be more appropriate for another of the same size.

8.7.3 Sheltered accommodation

This is designed for elderly people and those with disabilities who require some support and care, but who may be more able than those living in residential homes or nursing homes. Accommodation may be under one roof, or in bungalows with warden attendance and a nearby community room. The size of units can vary from fewer than 10 residents to 'villages' of several hundred. The take-up of service will vary from unit to unit, and a very flexible approach to service delivery must be employed. In order to deploy services economically and still meet the needs of residents adequately, an authority with a large number of units will employ bookbus, mobile, housebound library service to individuals and deposit collection in any combination that is appropriate.

8.8 *Conclusion*

People living in residential homes and sheltered accommodation, or attending day centres, require a library service which is appropriate to their needs. Contact with trained library staff is central to an adequate level of service. A wide range of services, materials, and reading aids should be provided. The method of service delivery should be appropriate to the needs of users. Visits should be regular and of a frequency that matches user needs.

9
STOCK

Introduction

Whether the service is centralized or decentralized, users must have available the same range of material as individuals using a community or mobile library. Users will not have access to a library collection and therefore rely on housebound library service staff to act as intermediaries between themselves and the stock of the library system. As library users, housebound people should not be stereotyped and care should be taken at the two main stages in selecting materials for them to use:

- purchasing of suitable material
- selecting from that stock prior to a visit to an individual.

9.1 *Stock selection objectives, policy and techniques*

9.1.1 The objective is to provide a stock suitable in presentation and content to satisfy the library requirements of the users.

9.1.2 Selection policy will be based, as with community libraries, on perceived and anticipated needs, and on issues and requests. It should also take into account different emphases and special requirements. The stock profile will change as the profile of users changes, but stock should promote a positive image of elderly people and those with disabilities.

9.1.3 It is vital to select stock from approvals rather than from order lists or slips in order to assess print size and quality and the presentation and weight of the volume.

9.2 *Who selects stock for purchase?*

9.2.1 In a centralized service it is preferable that stock should be selected by staff involved with the users on a daily basis.

9.2.2 In a decentralized service it is essential that housebound library service staff have an advisory role guiding the librarian from whose stock the materials will be drawn, as to particular needs, emphases and selection techniques. This should include regular attendance at stock selection meetings.

9.2.3 However the materials are selected, visitors must report back comments and changes in requirements to those responsible for stock purchase.

9.3 *Access to authority-wide stocks*

9.3.1 The housebound library service stock fund should be used to purchase materials for which a high demand is expected, or materials which are likely to be used primarily for housebound users.

9.3.2 In decentralized systems based in several libraries, some duplication of very popular material may be necessary to meet the needs of community and housebound users.

9.3.3 In both centralized and decentralized services it will be necessary to borrow from libraries and specialist stocks in order to cater for minority interests and specific requests.

9.4 *Range of materials needed*
The range of materials which must be available will include special formats, both in English and community languages, unlikely to be found in large quantities in community libraries. These should appeal to people from all cultural backgrounds. Some materials, such as some unabridged spoken word cassettes, can also be expensive. Items normally considered to be for reference only may need to be made available for loan.

Materials should include:

9.4.1 Books in ordinary print in English and community languages Wherever possible, these should be in clear print and be light to hold. Paperbacks should be included where suitable.

Fiction – with particular emphasis on the latest novels, genre fiction, standard works and reprints.

Non-fiction – with particular emphasis on the most heavily used categories.

9.4.2 Illustrated books
Heavily illustrated books are popular and attractive. If the text is in clear print, such material can also supplement large-print stocks or be of use to people with poor concentration.

9.4.3 Large print

Many people can only read large print, so stock should be wide ranging and include paperbacks, non-fiction and reference publications of minority large-print publishers. Librarians should be aware that large-print publishers use a variety of contrasts, layouts and print sizes and these variations can make a significant difference to people with a visual impairment. There is also a considerable amount of material available in clear print.

9.4.4 Spoken word cassettes

The range of material and number of titles should be extensive. The technical and artistic quality should be high, with good reproduction. Titles of differing lengths should be selected, including abridged items, as they are useful for people with a short concentration span. Reference and information material is available on cassette and should be purchased where appropriate. The spoken word cassette stock can be extended by the use of other agencies who publish a wider range of books, talking newspapers and magazines. The librarian responsible for stock selection should ensure that these facilities are known to staff and users and are accessible where needed. For further information refer to Section 10 Reading aids and tape services.

9.4.5 Music

Music may be the main interest of some users. Cassettes are currently the most popular format but vinyl LPs and compact discs should be provided. Music videos could also be considered for stock or borrowed from another section.

Some printed music scores are produced in larger type for visually impaired people.

9.4.6 Videos

The range of videos currently available is extensive, including educational and leisure titles, some of which are available in subtitled and signed formats.

9.4.7 Reminiscence material

There is a range of reminiscence material in different formats produced by specialist publishers, including slides and videos. Photographs, albums, local scenes and scrapbooks, can also be purchased or assembled by staff.

9.4.8 Special materials for adults with limited literacy skills

Adults with limited literacy skills and pre-lingually deaf people will need easy reading material; people with learning difficulties will need social/life skills material; stroke patients will need material to help them re-learn communication skills; elderly mentally confused people can benefit from reality orientation resources. Useful information on stock for people with learning difficulties is contained in *Library services to housebound people.*[9]

9.4.9 Materials for staff in organizations, parents and carers

Stock should include literature on disability and specific conditions, and materials on ideas for activities including quiz books, song cassettes and reminiscence resources. Publications giving information about local and national services and relevant organizations should also be included.

9.4.10 Computer software

Educational software, including distance-learning resources, is being developed and people who are housebound could derive great benefit from this material.

9.4.11 Periodicals

Many users enjoy browsing through periodicals which may also provide a useful supplement to other areas of stock. Periodicals should be up to date and may need to be purchased for the housebound library service.

9.4.12 Jigsaws

Jigsaws should vary in size and complexity. All pictures should be appropriate for adults. Wooden ones last longer and are helpful for people with restricted movement in their hands.

9.4.13 Picture loans

This service may be enjoyed by people who are housebound. If a library service provides this service the loan period could be longer for housebound users and catalogues should be made available to borrowers at home.

9.5 *Selection for the user*

There are two usual methods:

- pre-selecting all items at the base library
- taking boxes of relevant material from which the user selects.

They differ mainly in where the greatest proportion of staff time is spent, and in the size of the base stock from which the final selection is made.

9.5.1 Pre-selecting all items at the base library

Pre-selection takes place from a wide base stock for an individual, with a detailed user profile. This method will also involve procedures which prevent material being sent repeatedly to the same person, and more complicated packing systems.

9.5.2 Taking boxes of relevant material from which the user selects
Selection takes place from a wide base stock for a group of users, with a group profile. Materials are packed into boxes according to genre or category and the library visitor takes an appropriate selection into the person's home, where the final choice is made. The system should be flexible enough to cater for minority needs and special interests. Users must be able to request specific titles and types of materials not usually included in the boxes. This method involves more stock in delivery routines but should not affect overall issues. There may be a psychological advantage for the user in being able to make the final selection.

9.5.3 Pre-selecting all items seems to be the most effective for user satisfaction and for the optimum deployment of stock. Pre-selecting all items involves more time at the base library; taking boxes of materials requires more time with the user while the final selection is made.

9.5.4 The method of selection may be affected by other factors. These may include whether:

- the service is centralized or decentralized
- an individual or an institution is being served
- volunteers are involved in deliveries.

9.5.5 The user profile must be referred to during the selection process and must be updated as required after each visit. The language or content of some stock may cause offence to some people and staff should be sensitive to their wishes. It is important that the terms used to describe stock are understood by both the visitor and the selector. For more detail on the user profile see Section 6.1.4.

9.5.6 Users need access to information about books and other material. This may be achieved by lists of new additions and subject lists in appropriate formats.

9.5.7 Feedback resulting from consultation with users should be given to publishers and suppliers, especially when requested material is not available.

9.6 *Number of items per user*
Users should be provided with sufficient material to last between one visit and the next.

9.7 *Issue system*
It is necessary to use a selection or issuing method which will avoid users being given the same material more than once, which is frustrating for the recipient and time-wasting for staff. Various methods can be used, from simple names or numbers on the date label to extensive computer records. The needs of the housebound library service should be incorporated when computer systems are developed. Inappropriate system-wide limits and routines may be triggered unless computer programs accommodate housebound library service loan periods and permitted numbers of items on loan.

Whichever method is used it must be flexible enough to cope with duplicate titles and different methods of selection for users.

10
READING AIDS AND TAPE SERVICES

Introduction

A wide variety of reading aids has been developed to enable people with disabilities to read printed material. They range from very simple devices to sophisticated, expensive equipment. The use of an aid enables the disabled reader to continue to read printed material. Alternative material in taped form should be provided if the reader does not wish to use an aid, or if there is no suitable aid available.

10.1 *Reading aids*

Reading aids fall broadly into two categories:

- those designed to enhance vision
- those designed to enable users with a physical disability to hold a book and turn pages.

10.1.1 Vision aids include a very wide range of magnifiers for different situations and different degrees of visual disability. Hand-held magnifiers, illuminated models and magnifiers which leave the hands free are simple to use. Electronic aids such as Viewscan and CCTV (closed-circuit television magnifier) are sophisticated items of equipment designed for people with high degrees of visual impairment. Poor vision can often be improved by effective local lighting. The provision of a reading lamp, with the light angled on the page, may provide sufficient illumination. Attention should also be given to the natural light available. Net curtains should be avoided and the reader's chair positioned to take advantage of the maximum available light, avoiding glare.

10.1.2 Aids for people with physical disabilities include bookrests, prismatic spectacles which allow a supine person to read comfortably, and page turners. A page turner may range from a rubber thimble to enable a person whose grip is weak to turn pages, to an electronic model connected to a Possum environmental control system used by a person with a severe disability.

10.1.3 Information about reading aids

There is a range of published information which is required reading for any librarian working with housebound readers. The Partially Sighted Society provides a telephone information service on aids as well as a published list of detailed product information which is regularly updated.[10] A product guide which also gives valuable information and guidance in the selection of equipment is published by the Oxfordshire Health Authority.[11] The BBC's *In touch* guide to services to people with a visual handicap is particularly useful for its coverage of aids and tape services.[12] A very helpful introduction to the use of reading aids in libraries, tape services, and services to people with visual disabilities will be found in *Library services to housebound people.*[13]

10.1.4 Contact with other agencies

The librarian should have a knowledge of local agencies where help and advice can be sought, and where readers can be referred for the appropriate aid for specific disabilities. These will include opticians, ophthalmologists, low vision clinics, Social Services Departments and rehabilitation units and the librarian should be aware of the range and extent of the local services, and seek to develop contacts with them. A knowledge of the national agencies concerned with disability, and the services they provide, is essential. Reference should be made to Section 11 Liaison with agencies, for further information.

10.1.5 The librarian's role in the provision of reading aids

- The librarian should have a working knowledge of reading aids and how and where they can be obtained.

- A preliminary assessment of the reader's requirements should be made. It must be emphasized that if these are beyond the scope of a basic aid, such as a book stand or simple page turner, the reader should be referred to a professional agency where expert advice and assistance can be given. If the reader has a visual disability, for example, then referral should be made to an optician or ophthalmologist who will prescribe the most appropriate magnifying aid. If a page turner is required, then the reader should be referred to an occupational therapist in the Social Services Department.

- The referral could be made to the appropriate agency by the librarian, with the prior consent of the reader.

- When the aid has been obtained the librarian should show the reader how to use it, if this has not already been done by a therapist, and monitor its use to ensure its continued suitability.

10.2 *Taped materials and services*

10.2.1 Taped material should be provided for people who cannot read or handle a printed book and who cannot, or who may prefer not to, use an aid.

10.2.2 A wide range of material is available on tape, covering recreational and educational material, and community information, broadly comprising the following categories:

- talking books on compact cassette from commercial publishers
- talking newspapers, local and national
- taped magazines
- taped information published by local and national organizations
- material from the national tape lending libraries, for example RNIB Talking Book Service, RNIB Cassette Library, Calibre, National Listening Library.

10.2.3 Information about tape services
The Talking Newspaper Association of the United Kingdom (TNAUK) is the main source of information on tape services. It produces a directory of local and national services, including a list of taped newspapers and periodicals.[14]

10.2.4 The housebound library service should provide a wide range of talking books for visually impaired users, including those who may wish to use the local library service instead of, or in addition to, the national library services for visually impaired people and others with special needs. The librarian should have a good knowledge of local and national tape services to ensure the user's access to a wide range of suitable material.

10.2.5 The librarian's role in the provision of taped materials

- The librarian should ensure that sufficient taped material is available for the user's needs. The user should be informed of the services available, and should be put in touch if required with local and national talking newspapers, music resources, sources of taped information, and other tape services.

- A cassette player, on short or long loan, should be provided if required. The machine should be sturdy and simple to operate. The controls should be identifiable through tactile means if the person is visually impaired. The user should be shown how to operate it. Time spent at this stage helping the user to become familiar with the controls will prevent frustration which may result in a disinclination to use this method of 'reading'.

- Referrals to tape services should be made by the librarian with the prior consent of the user. The use and satisfaction level should be monitored and problems experienced by the user should be taken up by the librarian, if requested, with the relevant service.

- A number of national tape library services require users to select a list of books from a printed catalogue, which they may be unable to read. The librarian is the most appropriate person to assist the user with the selection of material and should be prepared to do this.

10.3 *Provision of other formats of material*
While taped material is the format most likely to be required by visually impaired housebound people, there may be occasions when embossed print (Braille, Moon) will be needed. In order to give a satisfactory service the librarian should be knowledgeable about the provision of embossed material, and how it can be obtained.

11
LIAISON WITH AGENCIES

Introduction
The housebound library service is one of a range of services which contribute to the well-being of elderly people, those with disabilities and other clients in the community. It operates alongside many other agencies concerned with the provision of social, health, education, leisure and information services.

The policy of care in the community, which has seen people returning from institutions to their home communities, or continuing to live as long as possible in their own homes, has placed new demands on local service providers. The library service in general, and the housebound library service in particular, has a vital part to play in the development of a network of support to these people, and to those who work with them or care for them.

Cooperation with other agencies, whether on an informal basis or as part of a defined partnership, is essential if the housebound library service is to achieve its aims and enhance and improve its provision. Close and effective liaison will also allow these other agencies to improve aspects of their own service delivery.

11.1 *Purposes of liaison*
These include:

- recruitment of new users for the housebound library service
- publicizing specific library service projects and initiatives (for example, events)
- obtaining feedback on the effectiveness of the housebound library service
- finding out about, or obtaining, publications and information items
- recruitment of volunteers
- getting comments or advice on particular library materials
- making referrals of housebound library service clients to other agencies for services or information

- provision of direct services (for example, outreach collections of material to staff of agencies to allow them to develop their own work with clients)
- development of training initiatives.

11.2 *Range of agencies with which liaison is necessary*

Staff of the housebound library service should be aware of the wide range of relevant agencies providing services. In some cases, liaison will be close and continuous; in others, as required to answer a specific need (for example, referral to a specialist service).

Some of the most important of these agencies with which contact should be developed include:

11.2.1 Local statutory health and social services

- Social Services Department – for contact with local social workers, occupational and speech therapists, rehabilitation advisers, home helps, residential social workers and day centre staff, specialist social workers for visual and hearing impairment and mental health

- District Health Authority – medical social workers, staff of low vision clinics, early discharge teams, community psychiatric nurses

- GPs and Health Centres

11.2.2 Local voluntary agencies

- local branches of Age Concern, Pensioners' Link, Task Force and WRVS
- local associations for people with disabilities, Dial-a-Ride, MIND

11.2.3 Local education, recreation and information agencies

- Adult Education Institutes, especially community education workers
- local branches of the University of the Third Age and the Workers' Education Association
- local history societies
- local Departments of Leisure or Recreation, including community sports and arts officers
- DIAL (Disablement Information and Advice Line)
- Citizens' Advice Bureaux
- local Talking Newspaper groups

11.2.4 Local groups serving people with other special needs

- ethnic minority community organizations
- groups for older or disabled gay men and lesbians
- carers' support groups

11.2.5 National agencies

- Age Concern, Help the Aged, Centre for Policy on Ageing
- Disabled Living Foundation, RNIB, Partially Sighted Society, RNID, British Deaf Association, British Association of the Hard of Hearing, RADAR, Spastics Society, Alzheimer's Disease Society
- Association of Carers
- Talking Newspaper Association of the UK, RNIB Talking Book Service, National Listening Library, Feminist Audio Books

11.3 *Developing effective liaison*

11.3.1 Where another agency, such as the WRVS, is directly involved with the library service in the operation of the housebound library service, a clear policy framework will need to be jointly developed to define the aims and priorities of the service. Formal arrangements must be made in areas such as recruitment and training, stock selection, monitoring the quality of service and conditions of service for volunteers.

11.3.2 Staff of the housebound library service should ensure that all local agencies which are in contact with potential users are fully aware of the existence of the service, what it provides and the criteria for eligibility. Agencies should be provided with a supply of publicity materials and referral forms and be fully briefed on their use. Contact should be maintained to ensure that further supplies are provided as necessary.

Guidance on the development of a full programme of publicity and promotion is given in Section 12 Promotion and publicity.

11.3.3 Introductory talks should be given by housebound library service staff to groups of staff of other agencies, for example at their regular team or management meeting.

11.3.4 Similarly, the housebound library service should establish a system to ensure that it receives supplies of publicity materials and other information from other agencies to distribute to its users. Speakers from appropriate agencies should be invited to take part in induction training of library staff in areas such as those outlined in Section 5 Training.

11.3.5 Written records should be kept of significant contacts with other agencies (for example, reports of talks or training sessions given). An accurate information file giving contact details for all useful agencies and their key personnel should be maintained at the housebound library service base and, as required, in portable form for staff visiting users.

11.3.6 Details of specific referrals or enquiries made on behalf of users should be recorded and followed up to ensure that effective contact has been achieved.

11.3.7 Housebound library service staff should be involved in the planning of joint services to elderly people and those with disabilities in their areas, for example through cross-agency committees to plan new facilities or specific events.

11.3.8 Other agencies should be involved as fully as possible in specific library initiatives, for example in providing transport, facilities or speakers for library clubs.

11.3.9 Housebound library service staff should provide support for initiatives taken by other agencies, for example in publicizing to users events such as displays, shows and open days, and if necessary, in liaising over transport and other arrangements for individuals.

11.3.10 Staff of agencies with particular expertise should be asked to help with selection and promotion of stock, for example by accompanying librarians on buying visits to suppliers and contributing to stock selection meetings on specific topics.

12
PROMOTION AND PUBLICITY

Introduction

Promotion and publicity are fundamental to effective library services. Every visit to a user is an opportunity for staff to exploit the potential for advertising services, assessing user demands and responding to these where possible.

Promotion and publicity provide essential management information. They establish the nature and size of demand so that relevant objectives and policies can be pursued and resources allocated effectively.

Well-designed services must still be marketed to be successful, and in this role, promotion and publicity will be undertaken as a specific activity.

Central to promotion and publicity are questions of identifying demand, defining services and securing resources. Therefore, policy decisions about the current identity and future development of services must include discussion of these items.

12.1 *Promotion*

Promotion is best defined as an activity-based process to draw attention to, or to increase the profile of, library services. Promotion should be used to create a favourable environment for the service by developing and advertising an image which is positive, attractive to potential users and multi-ethnic. The use of a range of activities will illustrate specifically what the library service has to offer. Determining which groups to contact, where they are to be found, and what promotional material is most appropriate will dictate how and where promotion is undertaken.

12.1.1 Promotion to existing users
For example:

- booklists
- newsletters/magazines
- library talks   } to existing sites, locations
- displays/exhibitions
- library clubs.

65

Newsletters can promote stock by appending booklists and references to articles, and promote the enjoyment of literature with book reviews and encouragement for users to write poetry and stories for publication. Library clubs are another effective way of achieving this. An important element of library clubs is their social atmosphere, which can lead to the development of linked activities. However, housebound library service staff should liaise to ensure that the promotion of the library service remains a constant feature of the programme.

12.1.2 Direct promotion to attract new users
For example:

- information/benefits sessions
- library publications sales
- displays/exhibitions to new locations.

Information/benefits 'workshops' and library publications sales (perhaps organized as a 'coffee morning' event) can be a good way of attracting new custom at existing sites or of introducing at new sites (for example, a multicultural day centre) the range of services available.

12.1.3 Promotion in the community through joint library activities
For example:

- transporting deposit collections for young people's services
- working with community services on outreach to ethnic minorities
- cooperation with archives/local history sections on reminiscence work in old people's clubs.

Exploiting a corporate approach to transport use and project work will provide opportunities for promotion in communities not normally aware of housebound library services.

12.1.4 Cooperative promotion with other agencies, statutory and voluntary
For example:

- authority shows/festivals
- joint services
- community events/festivals
- local events by particular groups.

Authority shows/festivals are an essential opportunity for promotion, presenting the chance to offer either basic service information, or a specific display to link into a theme. Joint services (for example, to a centre, with an outreach sports team) are a powerful way of increasing impact and response. Participation in local/group festivals and events is an opportunity not only for broad or thematic displays and exhibitions, but also for promoting the resources of the library service by discovering and assisting the groups' requirements for halls for hire, reprographic equipment and other facilities.

12.2 *Publicity*

Publicity, i.e. printed material or broadcast information, is a fundamental part of promotional activity. To be produced successfully, it must answer the questions 'who do you want to reach?', 'why do you wish to contact them?', 'where are they?', 'how are you to contact them?'. It should always be part of budget calculations, whether the capital costs of a new development or the revenue expenditure of existing services.

12.2.1 Programme

The publicity programme will vary enormously in extent, form and media for distribution according to:

- target, for example new service, new users for existing service
- coverage, for example authority-wide/local
- client group, for example users – potential or existing
  - elderly people
  - ethnic minority elders
  - young people with disabilities
  - contact groups
  - carers/relations
  - home helps.

12.2.2 Distribution

To facilitate the completion of whichever programme is required, it is important that the housebound library service reaches users by establishing links with other agencies and their clients, some of which will be used continually, others for a specific purpose. Among those it is essential to consider are:

- library/leisure services (constant display)
- authority staff (social services, housing induction training)
- local hospitals (patients' information booklet)
- community health centres
- places of religious worship

- groups working with/on behalf of elderly people (Age Concern)
- tenants' organizations
- community/ethnic groups
- housing associations
- pensioners' associations
- local shopping centres
- ethnic minority shops
- clubs/societies for people with disabilities (DIAL and others)
- transport services (Dial-a-Ride, etc.)
- advice centres (Citizens' Advice Bureaux).

12.2.3 Form and medium

Consideration of the needs and characteristics of the client group will affect the choice of form (production in print, tape or oral format), language used, and medium.

Among media to be considered are:

- local newspapers, including free press and the authority's own paper
- ethnic publications
- tenants'/estate newsletters
- community and voluntary newsletters
- local radio
- local hospital radio
- posters and leaflets
- mobile display
- tape-slide presentations
- talks
- direct mail to addresses on Social Services Departments' registers of people with disabilities.

12.2.4 Content and production

The image of any publicity material will share an identity established by the local authority guidelines, but effective publicity to housebound library service users should emphasize:

- the availability of services, not restrictions on them
- the wide range of people who can be considered eligible for the service
- access to the totality of the library service.

Given this brief, it may well be best to produce a series of publicity items. Linked by a common logo, appearance or theme, each piece of publicity should avoid excessive detail and be easy to understand, with:

- a text that uses clear language throughout
- a text that works in more than one form (for example, print and tape)
- a text that is available in all of the main languages spoken locally
- a simple text that is suitable for translation as required
- a section that invites or allows for response.

Where the format is print, a good-sized typeface and contrast should be used to maximize legibility.

All publicity should avoid the use of ageist, racist or sexist stereotypes, or a text that could in any way be interpreted as offensive or patronizing.

12.3 Promotion and publicity are both basic and essential to the operation of successful services, and a full programme should include monitoring, feedback and evaluation.

13
TRANSPORT

Introduction

Decisions about vehicles are of great strategic importance for a housebound library service. Whether a vehicle is purchased through capital outlay or a leasing scheme it is, once acquired, the long-term basis of the service infrastructure. A vehicle should be designed with due consideration of the likely expansion of services.

Many secondary decisions also need to be taken about the management of transport to ensure its successful use and smooth operation.

13.1 *Choice of vehicle*

13.1.1 Range

There are several types of vehicle which are currently in use:

- goods van, rear access/internal access from integral cab
  suitable for use by up to three members of staff, or on longer routes which require larger loads, or as a delivery vehicle carrying, for example, deposit collections

- small van/estate car
  likely to be used by one to two members of staff, or on shorter routes, or where limited load capacity is adequate

- custom-built mobile
  a smaller vehicle of this type might be in use exclusively with the housebound section to serve individuals, sheltered accommodation and residential homes. A valuable feature of a small mobile is that access at any identified site is unlikely to be a problem. A larger vehicle in use with the authority as a standard mobile might have a percentage of its working time committed to the housebound library service which, in this case, is possibly decentralized

- multi-purpose vehicle
  this is a vehicle in use on housebound routes, with variable internal

space, which by the removal or addition of seating could be used to deliver deposit collections, or to transport users to libraries and activities

- privately owned vehicles
used by staff or volunteers receiving mileage allowance.

13.1.2 Factors which will influence the choice of vehicle to be deployed are:

- cost and efficiency
- load to be carried (number of users on a route, frequency of visit and method of stock selection)
- staff complement (maximum agreed staffing level)
- local environment (urban/rural, parking, congestion, security problems)
- compatibility with the existing fleet vehicles of the local authority.

13.2 *Equipping the vehicle*

Different methods of selection require materials to be separated to different degrees. At the very least, the vehicle should be fitted with a flat, smooth floor. For flexibility, safety and ease of use, it may be advisable to fit the vehicle with racking or shelving which should be completely removable and adaptable for multi-media storage.

13.3 *Facilities*

13.3.1 Staff facilities must take into account health and safety requirements and the working needs of employees who may be obliged to spend long hours in the vehicle. Features may include:

- first aid kit
- fire extinguisher
- fire escape route/hatch
- supplementary heating/fan (auxiliary battery possibly needed)
- supplementary lighting
- personal storage
- washbasin
- radio/phone.

13.3.2 Public facilities that must be provided where it is expected that users will enter the vehicle include:

- shallow steps/ramp/wheelchair lift
- non-slip floor
- grab handles
- courtesy seating
- standard seating, suitably finished and equipped (headrests, seatbelts), if the vehicle is to be used to transport people to a library
- all shelving at convenient height
- good lighting and signing.

13.4 *Finishing*

A vehicle's finishing determines the extent to which it is recognizable and identifiable. This will be influenced by:

- choice of corporate or individual livery and logo
- signwriting/legend
- how far an anonymous vehicle will best serve users by not drawing attention to vulnerable housebound people
- use of external noticeboards on larger vehicles and mobiles
- provision of klaxon or horn to announce arrival at site.

13.5 *Vehicle operation*

13.5.1 In the case of privately owned vehicles, line managers must ensure that both staff and volunteers, either individually or through their agency, are reimbursed with a mileage allowance and covered by insurance.

13.5.2 Driving

The provision of the driving resource is integral to service delivery. The quality of the service can be greatly improved if the driving element is managed to give reliability, continuity and cover and developed to contribute local knowledge and awareness of service requirements.

For these reasons it is preferable that drivers should be under the control of the library service and not from an isolated transport pool.

Once this has been established, there is the question of whether the service should operate with a separate driver from library manual staff, a librarian-driver, a library staff-driver or volunteer driver. This will be influenced by the organization of the service and local circumstances, and factors involved will include, for example, the size of the vehicle, traffic congestion and ease of parking. However, consideration of these items must be subject to achieving the main objectives of the service, that a professional or trained person is free to provide the required library services to users without hindrance, and that a driver is gainfully employed for the optimum amount of time.

The provision of training in driving skills is essential. Staff who already drive can extend their competence to drive specific vehicles. Moreover, non-drivers can be recruited with the requirement that they learn to drive. This gives maximum flexibility when organizing schedules and allows restructuring without losing valued staff.

13.5.3 Garaging
Secure garaging close to the housebound library service base is of prime importance in providing regular and reliable services.

13.5.4 Accident insurance
All staff must be fully informed of the procedures to follow in the event of an accident. For certain vehicles, special schemes such as minibus insurance may be found to be appropriate.

13.6 *Support services*

13.6.1 Maintenance and ownership
Whether the library vehicle is owned or leased it is essential that it is included in the programme of maintenance for the local authority's fleet, with arrangements made to include daily/weekly routines and interim and major mechanical servicing.

13.6.2 Vehicle replacement – temporary/short-term
It is essential that whenever the library vehicle is off the road, whether scheduled or due to an emergency, a relief vehicle is available to provide cover. However, all that can be expected is that such a vehicle be well maintained and clean, and therefore the more specialized the library vehicle, the less adequately will the temporary vehicle be able to fill its role.

13.6.3 Vehicle replacement – permanent/long-term
Thought must be given to replacement strategies which, given current trends in vehicle operation, are likely to be fleet management or leasing schemes.

14
HEALTH AND SAFETY

14.1 *Safety policy*

14.1.1 Housebound library service staff and volunteers often work in isolation and away from authority premises. The nature of their work, the conditions they work in and specific duties may make them more susceptible to illness and/or injury than building-based staff.

14.1.2 The local authority's Safety Policy, as required by the Health and Safety at Work Act 1974 and related legislation, must be brought to the attention of individuals working outside library buildings, guidelines produced on specific working practices to avoid injury, and appropriate training given.

14.1.3 Housebound library service staff have little control over the environment they work in, but they do have a responsibility for their own health and safety at work. For this reason, staff and volunteers should be issued with general and specific advice on identifying and coping with hazards at work.

14.2 *Lifting and carrying*

14.2.1 Proper instruction must be given in respect of lifting and carrying stock, boxes and equipment. The need for care at all times, especially when entering buildings while carrying materials, should be stressed, and relevant publications should be given to all members of staff and volunteers.

Adequate equipment should be made available which suits the purpose of the procedures involved. Suitable containers which minimize physical strain should be provided.

14.2.2 Proper instruction should be given on handling and pushing wheelchairs, and assisting people with disabilities in and out of vehicles and around buildings.

14.3 *Clothing*

Staff who are engaged in visiting for a substantial part of their duties should be provided with protective clothing and footwear.

14.4 *Equipment*

Suitable equipment will be necessary for staff and volunteers, although what is appropriate may vary between individuals. Trolleys, boxes, bags should be provided in sufficient quantity for the number of visitors making deliveries at one time. Equipment should be strong and easy to handle, not too heavy, and suitable for use in all weather.

All equipment should be selected by staff with safety in mind.

14.5 *Vehicles*

14.5.1 Vehicles should be properly maintained and clean, and suit the purpose for which they are used. Inadequate or poorly fitted or equipped vehicles could prove a health and safety hazard for users. If a vehicle is one intended for public use, entrances and layout must comply with established guidelines for public safety. See also Section 13 Transport.

14.5.2 Fire extinguishers and first aid boxes must be carried and checked regularly.

14.5.3 Vehicles must be included in the health and safety inspections which are carried out at the workplace and arrangements made to facilitate this.

14.6 *Stress*

Line managers must be aware of potential stress factors in work carried out by staff and volunteers and be sensitive to individual responses. Proper support structures must be devised to avoid the buildup of occupational stress wherever possible. In the interests of staff engaged on regular visiting duties, workloads must be carefully monitored. Guidelines outlined in Section 4 Staffing should be followed to avoid inappropriate workload for individuals.

14.7 *Personal security*

14.7.1 Staff and volunteers should receive guidance and advice on coping with difficult or dangerous situations while travelling or visiting particular areas or establishments. It may be necessary to enlist the help of other professionals in giving advice, for example the mental health team, Social Services staff or the police.

14.7.2 It may be necessary to send staff or volunteers in pairs to certain areas for their own protection. Personal alarms of the type which leave hands free should be issued where appropriate and consideration given to installing radio/telephone links in vehicles.

14.7.3 Sexual or racial harassment may be a problem for some staff and should be taken very seriously by managers. Proper lines of referral and support must be established for staff and volunteers who are affected.

14.7.4 Personal identity cards should be issued to all staff and volunteers who make visits to housebound users.

14.8 *First aid*
Staff should be aware of the first aid policy of the authority, and whom to contact in cases of emergency such as hypothermia.

14.9 *Accidents and insurance*

14.9.1 Staff and volunteers making visits to housebound users are vulnerable to accidents due to the nature of the work. Some authorities provide additional insurance cover for employees at greater risk owing to the nature of the job they do, but staff should be aware that this will not apply if they are injured while carrying out inappropriate or non-library service related tasks.

Most authorities issue accident forms to record accidents at work. Procedures should be fully understood by staff and volunteers of the housebound library service. Accidents occurring during visits should be reported using the relevant forms. Procedures to be followed in the event of an accident should be clearly understood and available in written form in any vehicles used.

14.9.2 Staff using their own transport should arrange adequate insurance cover for business or professional use, and be reimbursed by their authority.

14.9.3 Volunteers should be properly insured, especially when using their own vehicle for deliveries. Many umbrella organizations provide cover at minimal cost for drivers engaged in voluntary work and these should be made available to volunteers carrying out visiting. Many schemes also exist for personal cover for volunteers.

15
ACCOMMODATION AND EQUIPMENT

15.1 *Accommodation*

15.1.1 Accommodation should be convenient, safe, pleasant to use and accessible to people with disabilities, to enable the housebound library service to carry out its functions effectively and efficiently. This applies both to a centralized service from a single location and to a decentralized service from a number of locations. Therefore, those involved in providing suitable accommodation need to have a clear understanding of the purpose and function of the service.

15.1.2 Siting and location need to take account of the organization and delivery of the service. The aim should be to provide a site which allows good access to library materials and easy loading of vehicles. Suitable parking spaces should be nearby. The location of the building should be convenient for access to all parts of the area being served.

15.1.3 Space and storage requirements will depend on the scale of the service. There must be sufficient space to accommodate staff. This should include a work area adequate for all staff duties, provision for counselling and interviewing, and rest facilities. There must be space for shelved stock and for storage of outgoing and incoming deliveries.

15.1.4 Internal layout and allocation of space should provide for ease of movement between tasks, logical workflow and a safe working environment. Clear signing, good lighting and non-slip, heavy-duty flooring are very important.

15.2 *Equipment*

15.2.1 Equipment can be divided into several groups – service equipment, office equipment and reading aids.

15.2.2 Service equipment is specific to the needs of the service. It includes trolleys, boxes and carrying aids and protective clothing.

15.2.3 Office equipment is necessary for the efficient functioning of the service, and will include desks, chairs, cupboards, lockers, noticeboards, telephone, Minicom, typewriter/word processor, computer issue and/or computer information terminals, photocopier, cassette players, stationery and publicity materials. Access to such equipment is necessary where not provided for the housebound library service.

15.2.4 Reading aids are described in Section 10 Reading aids and tape services. Secure storage should be provided for this equipment when not on loan.

APPENDIX 1
MEMBERSHIP OF THE WORKING PARTY

Members of the working party at September 1990

* Tom Berry, Special Services Librarian, London Borough of Hounslow Leisure Services

* Hugh Coffey, Hospitals and Housebound Librarian, London Borough of Hackney Leisure Services

** Carolyn Date, Domiciliary Services Librarian (East Area), Dorset County Libraries

** Jean Machell, Special Services Officer, Cleveland County Libraries and Leisure Department

** Julie Ryder (Convenor), Community Care Librarian, City of Westminster Education and Leisure Services

* Zia Siraj, Librarian, Mobile and Housebound Services, London Borough of Wandsworth Leisure and Amenity Services

* David Strong (Secretary), Principal Librarian Adult and Specialist Services, London Borough of Lambeth Amenity Services

Former member of the working party

** Diane Finlayson, formerly Housebound Librarian, London Borough of Southwark Leisure and Recreation Department (until July 1989)

** Nominees of the Domiciliary Services Subject Group
* Nominees of the London Housebound Services Group

REFERENCES

1 Library Association, *Guidelines for library provision in the Health Service. A consultative document*, Library Association, 1978. Reissued with amendments, 1980.

2 International Federation of Library Associations, Section of Library Services to Hospital Patients and Handicapped Readers, *Guidelines for libraries serving hospital patients and disabled people in the community*, IFLA, 1984 (IFLA Professional Report No. 2).

3 Local Authorities Management Services and Computer Committee (LAMSAC), *Staffing of public libraries: a report of the research undertaken by the Local Authorities Management Services and Computer Committee for the Department of Education and Science*, HMSO, 1976, 3 vols. (Library Information Series, No.7) Vol.3: Lewis, M. Joy, *Services to hospitals, to housebound readers and to institutions*, 1–89.

4 Library Association, *The use of volunteers in welfare libraries*, Library Association, 1987.

5 LAMSAC, op. cit., 46–9.

6 Ibid., 48–9.

7 Ryder, Julie (ed.), *Library services to housebound people*, Library Association, 1987, 195–200.

8 Kempson, Elaine and Dee, Marianne (eds.), *A future age: a practical handbook for librarians working with older adults*, Association of Assistant Librarians, 1987, 45–7.

9 Strong, David, 'Services to people with mental handicaps', in Ryder, Julie (ed.), op. cit., 160–84.

10 Details from the Low Vision Adviser, Partially Sighted Society, 105–109 Salusbury Road, London NW6 6RH (071-372 1551).

11 Southgate, T. N. (comp.), *Communication*, 7th ed., Oxfordshire Health Authority, 1990 (Equipment for Disabled People series).

12 Ford, Margaret and Heshel, Thena, *In touch: BBC Radio 4's guide to services for people with a visual handicap*, 7th ed., Broadcasting Support Services, 1990.

13 Burtrand, Dianne, 'Tape services'; Matthews, Graham, 'Reading aids'; Strong, David, 'Services to people with visual handicaps', in Ryder, Julie (ed.), op. cit., 102–10, 121–39, 151–9.

14 Talking Newspaper Association of the United Kingdom, *Guide to tape services for the handicapped*, 3rd ed., TNAUK, 1989.

SOURCES OF INFORMATION AND FURTHER READING

1 Library services

Clarke, Jean M. and Bostle, Eileen (eds.), *Reading therapy*, Library Association, 1988.

Clarke, Jean M. and Going, Mona (eds.), *Hospital libraries and community care*, 4th ed., Library Association, 1990.

Craddock, Peter, *The public library and blind people: a survey and review of current practice*, British Library, 1985 (LIR Report 36).

Dalton, Phyllis I., *Library service for the deaf and hearing impaired*, Oryx Press, 1985.

Health libraries review, quarterly, Blackwells Scientific Publications.

Hoy, Stephen and Sheila, *Reading for elderly people*, Winslow Press, 1987.

International Federation of Library Associations, Section of Library Services to Hospital Patients and Handicapped Readers, *Guidelines for libraries serving hospital patients and disabled people in the community*, IFLA, 1984 (IFLA Professional Report No.2).

Kempson, Elaine and Dee, Marianne (eds.), *A future age: a practical handbook for librarians working with older adults*, Association of Assistant Librarians, 1987.

Library Association, *Guidelines for library provision in the Health Service. A consultative document*, Library Association, 1978. Reissued with amendments, 1980.

Library Association, *The use of volunteers in welfare libraries*, Library Association, 1987.

Library Association, Medical, Health and Welfare Libraries Group, and Department of Library and Information Studies, Manchester Polytechnic, *Directory of domiciliary and hospital patients' library services in the United Kingdom*, Manchester Polytechnic, Department of Library and Information Studies, 1985.

Library Association, Medical, Health and Welfare Libraries Group, Domiciliary Services Subject Group, *Housecall*, twice-yearly.

Marshall, Margaret R., *Libraries and the handicapped child*, Andre Deutsch, 1981.

Marshall, Margaret R., Simonis-Rupert, Sancia, and Holst, Suzanne, *Books for the mentally handicapped: a guide to selection*, IFLA, 1983 (IFLA Professional Report No.1).

Pearlman, Della, *No choice. Library services for the mentally handicapped*, Library Association, 1982.

Ryder, Julie (ed.), *Library services to housebound people*, Library Association, 1987.

Turock, Betty J., *Serving the older adult. A guide to library programs and information sources*, Bowker, 1982.

Wigmore, Hilary, *The captive reader. A study of library services to the housebound in Harrow*, Cranfield Press, 1988.

2 Background information

Darnbrough, Ann and Kinrade, Derek, *Directory for disabled people*, 5th ed., Woodhead-Faulkner, 1988.

Darnbrough, Ann and Kinrade, Derek, *Directory for older people*, Woodhead-Faulkner, 1989.

Ford, Margaret and Heshel, Thena, *In Touch: BBC Radio 4's guide to services for people with a visual handicap*, 7th ed., Broadcasting Support Services, 1990.

Royal National Institute for the Deaf, *Information directory 1989–90*, RNID, 1989.

Southgate, T. N. (comp.), *Communication*, 7th ed., Oxfordshire Health Authority, 1990 (Equipment for Disabled People series).

Talking Newspaper Association of the United Kingdom, *Guide to tape services for the handicapped*, 3rd ed., TNAUK, 1989.